Dreamboats and Wishes

Emma Coates

Presentation by *BookLeaf Publishing*

Web: www.bookleafpub.com

E-mail: info@bookleafpub.com

ISBN: 9789357441148

First edition 2023

I'd like to dedicate this book to my wonderful partner and best friend, Phil. Without you by my side, this journey called life would not be the incredible, amazing and exciting ride it is. And to Bailey Boo - our 'best boy'. You are both my entire world.

And finally, to our precious love. Forever in our hearts, if not our arms:

'We loved you once, we love you still.

We always have, we always will.'

ACKNOWLEDGEMENT

The first poem I clearly remember writing was some twenty-plus years ago. It was a poem for my Nan, after the loss of her brother, and it was a defining moment for me. It was the moment I first understood what loss meant to people, and also the moment I realised I was quite good at writing poetry! The praise and encouragement I received from that one poem were all I needed to inspire me to write more. And with that in mind, I'd like to thank those people - my main supporters from day one. My family.

I'd also like to thank my primary school teachers - all of whom sparked my interest in creativity and writing.

To my fellow friends and members of 'The Invisible Tutor Group' - thank you for your support and encouragement over the past couple of years.

And last, but by no means least, thanks to Jim Hall - poet extraordinaire. Your wonderful online Zoom course came into my life at the perfect time last year, and your words of support and encouragement both at the time - and since - have been wonderful.

PREFACE

Since I was a little girl I have always read, enjoyed, and written poetry. Doing so has helped me through many stages of life - both good and bad - and rewards me with a huge sense of accomplishment and achievement when complete. A poem can take moments or hours to write, but always offers a lifetime of enjoyment and memories for years to come.

I hope you'll enjoy reading my collection as much as I have enjoyed writing it!

Dreamboats and Wishes

Dreamboats and wishes,
And New Year's kisses,
Under the mistletoe.

A brand new page,
As we take to the stage,
In life's own musical show.

Under moonlight,
Stars shine bright,
There's wondrous laughter and cheer.

New dreams begin,
As we chorus 'chin, chin!'
And wish all a Happy New Year!

'We'

We drink out in the gardens,
We drink out in the square,
We drink out in the sunshine,
We drink and we don't care.

We dance upon the moonbeams,
We dance upon the clouds,
We dance upon the rooftops,
We dance when we're not allowed.

We smile when we are dancing,
We smile when we have a drink,
We smile at all the memories,
We smile and we have a think.

We think about the good times,
We think about the bad,
We think about the happiness,
We think about the sad.

We share the wonderful moments,
We share, do you and me,
We share the laughter and the tears,
We share a life of glee!

Decorations

What is it about the decorations,
We save for special celebrations?
Christmas, New Year, and Easter too,
Valentine's and birthdays, a ghostly Halloween
boo.

What is it about the decorations,
We display without any hesitation?
They sparkle and glimmer on one's mantelpiece,
Endorphins and nostalgia, they always do
release.

What is it about the decorations,
We'd miss if we travelled on vacation?
Shiny baubles, twinkling lights, a fluffy tinsel
string,
The nativity on the windowsill, with the
new-born baby King.

It's the love they bring to the family home, year
upon good year,
The merriment of festive times, the warmth and
cosy cheer.
It's the memories that they behold, of many
times gone by.
The magic as we search above, in the Christmas
Eve night sky.

A New Year

4

The ice upon the rooftops,
The frost upon the lawn.
The world is fresh and quiet,
On this New Year's morn.

Sun bright above the clouds,
The rain has disappeared.
The year ahead excites us all,
Despite those things we feared.

Singing With Joy

5

Singing from the rooftops,
Singing from the trees,
Singing in the sunshine,
Singing through the breeze.

Singing with the girls,
Singing with the boys,
Singing with laughter,
Singing with joy.

A New Love

A new love dawned,
With roses and thorns,
And magic that wouldn't run smooth.

Love and laughter,
Happy ever after,
Each-other's hearts they will soothe.

For in each new day,
They'll always find a way,
To love through the tears and pain.

And through each dark night,
Every argument and fight,
The sunshine will outdo the rain.

Summer

Sunshine beams over the mountain-side,
Bees and butterflies no longer hide,
When summer awakens at last.

Birds tweet gaily,
While buttercups and daisies,
Swathe the meadows with a blast.

The gentle breeze blows,
Yet nobody knows,
What the whisper of the tree does say.

Golden rays reach,
The sand at the beach,
And in the waves, the children do play!

Wild Wilderness

Wild winds roar through the whimpering
wilderness,
Fierce like the dragon,
Its breath a savage beast.
Howling, tumbling, crashing into the earth.
Beating, breaking, bashing, mother nature's
birth.

Feral fragments of God's own mind,
Leave nothing but destruction behind.
Until the wilderness whimpers no more,
Never losing its own war.

Instead, it breathes, and rises above,
If only to show its true love.
The wild wilderness is here to stay,
The wild wilderness will not go away.

Stars

Up above the moonlit stars,
Is where I dream you'll be.
Up above the moonlit stars,
A little part of me.

We never held you in our arms,
Instead, you have flown free.
We never held you in our arms,
It wasn't meant to be.

My heart, it broke, into two,
The day you said goodbye.
My heart, it broke, into two,
Kept asking myself why.

But the world moves on,
And the stars, they shine.
But the world moves on,
And so must mine.

Butterflies and Daisies

Butterflies and daisies and dancing sunflowers,
Down through The Mumbles and onto The
Gower.
Y Ddraig Coch, it rises - with fire in its belly,
This one's for real - not just for the telly!
The passion of music - he sings from the heart,
His love for his country - a wondrous fine art.
Golden, the colour, of spring's daffodils,
Luscious and green, are its rolling hills.
In the Land of the Fathers, the seasons do shine,
Mystical and magical, is this homeland of mine.

Time

They wished they'd gone to school that day,
Instead of skipping class.
That they hadn't wished their lives away,
Or longed for time to pass.
For time is precious, they now know,
They cannot get it back.
And the lessons they learn, as they grow,
Are never white and black.
The sun appears, as does the rain,
Life itself is tough.
It's filled with laughter and with pain,
The good times and the rough.
But when they reach the end, my dear,
And reflect on all they've done.
They must remember the love and cheer,
The smiles and the fun.

Weather

The sun through the valleys,
A blaze of fire.
Its beams not for keeps,
Only for hire.

The rain in the orchard,
A blessing, it's true.
A drink for the fruits,
Their own special brew.

The snow on the mountains,
A picture so pretty.
Oh, how it glistens,
Like the lights in the city.

The wind through the forest,
The branches, they creak.
Whispering secrets,
The trees, they do speak.

The ice on the pathways,
Does sparkle and shine.
Christmas trees in windows,
The fresh scent of pine.

The hail on the rooftops,
In the dark of night.
Gives all those asleep,
A terrible fright.

You'll always take the weather with you,
Wherever you may go.
Whether sun, wind or rain,
Or hail, or ice or snow!

Because Of You

14

When the sun shines on my heart,
It melts the blues away.
When the sun shines on my life,
I hear the people say:
'You look so very happy,
Your smile, it does look true.'
And so I smile and tell them,
It's all because of you.

Clouds

Standing tall above the clouds is where I'd like
to be.
Standing tall above the clouds, higher than the
apple tree.
For the world, when seen from way up high, is
as pure as water's blue,
For the world, when seen from way up high, is
the place for me and you!

Garden Flowers

Roses are red,
Violets are blue.
Poems I write,
And this one's for you.

Pansies are purple,
Marigolds yellow.
I'm proud to call you,
My own handsome fellow.

Gerberas are orange,
Carnations are pink.
Sometimes your butt,
Really does stink!

Grasses are green,
Lillies are white.
Are you eating chocolate?
Ooo - give me a bite!

The Good Things In Life

Puppies and kittens,
Like soft, cosy mittens,
Are warm like a fluffy wool-coat.

Lambs and sweet bunnies,
Whose bounces are funny,
In springtime, oh how they do gloat.

Chenille, silk and satin,
When they touch on my bare skin,
Their softness I do love to feel.

The good things in life,
Without trouble or strife,
Bring a peace that is ever so real.

A Man's Best Friend

A lonely man called Bill,
Who lived upon the Moors,
Was angry with the world,
And Barnsley's footy scores.

Raging about the TV,
The price of ruddy fuel,
Nurses striking from their jobs,
Megan Markle's latest jewel.

It was no wonder he was lonely,
The way that he went on.
It was enough to scare the women off,
The likes of Betty John.

He'd started dating Karen,
But she soon told him straight.
'If it wasn't for your whinging ways,
You could be bloody great!'

'You look so tall and handsome,
Your arms, they feel so strong.
But the words that escape from your mouth,
Are never a tuneful song!'

'You're miserable and grumpy,
Your company isn't nice,
You've moaned and moaned for far too long,
And now you'll pay the price!

Now, lonely Bill felt pity,
Of his own self-loathing ways,
Vowed to hide away from everyone,
For the rest of his living days.

Until he met old Janey,
Walking through the muddy Moors.
She leapt up into his strong arms,
And dirtied his clean floors.

She flourished him with love,
In sun or rain or gale.
Whenever she did see him,
She wagged her fluffy tail.

A man's best friend is a dog,
He'd heard the people say,
But he never had believed it,
Until that very day!

An Apple A Day

'An apple a day keeps the doctor away.'
I was told as a little girl.
'Eat the crusts of your bread,
To give your hair a curl.'

'Actions speak louder than words.'
Is what my mother said,
Before she told me to put down my toys,
And head on up to bed.

'Absence makes the heart grow fonder.'
They said when he left for Spain,
But little did they know,
We'd never see him again.

'All that glitters, is not gold.'
My father said to me,
But I wouldn't listen to his words,
No, for myself, I had to see.

'All's fair in love and war.'
I told my sister so,
When I took the sweet she stole from me,
And threw it in the snow.

'Birds of a feather, flock together.'
The choir ladies sang.
When they took me under their own wings,
Welcomed me to their gang.

'Don't count your chickens, before they hatch.'
My Nana used to shout,
Then she grabbed my Gramps by the neck,
And chucked the bugger out!

'Fortune favours the bold.'
My boss said in his speech,
But I've yet to see it,
To me, it's yet to reach!

'People in glass houses,
Shouldn't be throwing stones!'
Is what the neighbour said to me,
Her name was Mrs Jones.

'Two wrongs just don't make a right.'
Said little Tommy Tipper.
How he knew, I'll never know,
For he was just a nipper!

The proverbial words you hear today,
Will live on Earth forever.
And though there's some you've yet to hear,
It's better late than never!

Love V Hate

How the love...

...soars through the hearts of the young.
...plays with time.
...spills out of our mouths in a moment.
...teases our body and mind.
...fuels us with passion, fire and warmth.
...changes through the journey of life.
...tinkers the beauty of the world.
...sparkles in the sunshine.
...glistens under the moonlight.
...Hurts.

How the hate...

...soars through the hearts of the young.
...plays with time.
...spills out of our mouths in a moment.
...teases our body and mind.
...fuels us with passion, fire and warmth.
...changes through the journey of life.
...tinkers the beauty of the world.
...snarls in the sunshine.
...glares under the moonlight.
...Hurts.

How the world is fuelled by both.

How our hearts burst and break.

How love versus hate.

Gratitude

I am happy
again. It's a wonderful feeling,
to feel nothing but happiness. The sunshine,
as it casts its golden glow on the
garden...the world. My life. The trees, suddenly
with
luscious green leaves. Where did
they come from? How did they appear? The
sweet twittering of
birdsong so near. With warmth
in my heart, and utterings of love. I look up,
and reach above.
Clouds...clouds have appeared, but the
golden rays shine through. Stronger than the
darkness.
Just like me and you,

On A Crisp Winter's Day

25

The sun shines brightly,
With the winter's glow,
Over the rooftops,
Glistening the snow.

The land has a sparkle,
So happy and gay,
Only to be seen,
On a crisp winter's day.

9 789357 441148